AF479373

FILM POEMS

REDELL OLSEN

LES FIGUES PRESS

Los Angeles

Film Poems
FIRST EDITION

Text design by Les Figues Press

ISBN 13: 978-1-934254-51-6
ISBN 10: 1-934254-51-7
Library of Congress Control Number: 2013952555

Les Figues Press thanks its subscribers for their support and readership. Les Figues Press is a 501c3 organization. Donations are tax-deductible.

Les Figues would like to acknowledge the following individuals for their generosity: Peter Binkow and Johanna Blakley, Lauren Bon, Elena Karina Byrne, Chris and Diane Calkins, Sarah de Heras, Pam Ore, Coco Owen, Dr. Robert Wessels, and the Skyscrape Foundation.

Les Figues Press titles are available through:
Les Figues Press, <http://www.lesfigues.com>
Small Press Distribution, <http://www.spdbooks.org>

Special thanks to Chelsea McNay, Marlan Sigelman, Julian Smith-Newman, Camille Thigpen, and Emerson Whitney.

TrenchArt 8/2

Book 3 of 5 in the TRENCHART Logistics Series.

This project is supported in part by a generous grant from the National Endowment for the Arts.

Post Office Box 7736
Los Angeles, CA 90007
info@lesfigues.com
www.lesfigues.com

CONTENTS

SELVAGE, RAFTS, AND PEACHES: REDELL OLSEN'S *FILM POEMS*

This book brings together five poetic sequences, proposing film poems as the compound title—genre even—for these different texts. We might take the title more as a flag of convenience, and move directly to the particulars and materials of each sequence. On the other hand, noting the risk of conflating different poems, we might also read the title as a conceptual manifesto, a call to re-orient image-text relations in contemporary poetics. Wittily indeterminate, the different formal mixes in *Film Poems* suggest new relations for film, performance, and poetry.

Part of the resonance and delight of film-poem as the relevant genre or compound concept for these poems is this play of relations between media. These are not poems that somehow illustrate or amplify stable references to film. The films that co-ordinate these texts are films made or remade by Olsen herself as film-texts rather than as homages to cinema or the Hollywood firmament. Her earlier poems include inter-medial interventions into our cinematic imaginations. 'Corrupted by Showgirls' in *Secure Portable Space* (2004), for example, re-animates the narrative grammar of noir femininity. In *Film Poems*, the textual syntax owes less to cinematic narratives, and more to film's frame rates and the syntax of image correlations.

Put crudely, Olsen's films don't do narrative realism, actors doing dialogue, all that kind of thing. Her essay on the poetics of the swoon in the film poetics of Abigail Child suggests some perspectives on her own aesthetics. Along with Abigail Child, a fondness for Matthew Barney's *Cremaster Cycle* is evident in Olsen's recent book *Punk Faun*. In search of other precedents, not least to articulate the fragility of film's performance, one might cite Robert Smithson's slide lecture *Hotel Palenque* (1972) or Victor Burgin's *Between* (1986). In Olsen's work, however, the conceptual weave is distinctive in its emphasis on poetry. Her films rarely use the soundtracks of found film materials, preferring to create a soundscape that can exist independently, whether as printed text or in performance, and so as film poems.

Some of the moves from poetry to film bear comparison with works such as Marcel Broodthaers's *Voyage on the North Sea*. In an interview, Broodthaers once remarked:

> I began with poetry, moved on to three-dimensional works, finally to film, which combines several artistic elements. That is, it is writing (poetry), object (something three-dimensional), and image (film). The great difficulty lies, of course, in finding a harmony among these three elements.

Olsen's work prefers disjunctions between media over any kind of harmony: opening differences amid media rather than among elements thereby unified. Indeed, her films have a structuralist quality akin to the theory and practice of 1970s film, or what Stephen Heath once termed 'cinetext': 'At work in the structuration of the cinetext is an overdetermination of codes which found its intelligibility.' One imagines Olsen could make stylish neo-feminist movies—Jean-Luc Godard crossed with Agnès Varda—if anyone offered her the resources. But rather than wait for the call from Universal Pictures, she has got on with making numerous films with the technology and materials, often found footage, closer to hand.

Olsen's practice as a film-maker and performer can be glimpsed from her website *filmpoems.wordpress.com*. Her films are also film-texts for performance, films that co-exist with poems for a variety of screening contexts, from gallery spaces and installations to shopping malls and sheds. The essay by Olsen entitled 'To Quill At Film,' published in parallel by Les Figues in *Logistics: Aesthetics*, offers an indispensable introduction to the concrete materiality of the films for which these poems were written, while also dramatising the poetics engaged. What emerges is a practice of poetic research that offers unusually powerful incisions in the intertwining of aesthetics and politics.

In 'London Land Marks' (2007), for example, expressions of survival from a teach-yourself Arabic audiotape cut into the grammatically fragmented film stills that would celebrate Speaker's Corner in Hyde Park. The practice of historical research into her materials is the more prominent in 'A New Booke of Copies' (2009) and 'SPRIGS & spots' (2011-12), in which ruffs, quills, lace, whitework and textiles of various kinds are investigated, remade or re-purposed. There are aspects of the resulting poetics that suggest critical analogies with Susan Howe, whose essay on Chris Marker emphasizes montage conflicts and the ideogram as a construction parameter in Eisenstein's materialism of cinema. Olsen's work is persistently engaged with the montage of materials and material relations, but also, especially as compared with Susan Howe's poetry, with a grittier, less minimalist conceptuality that is more troubled by its delighted complicity with art and culture, including what is still rather awkwardly known as popular culture. 'The Lost Pool' tribute to Esther Williams, for example, and the replay of daft ghillie suit wearers in 'Bucolic Picnic' both suggest satire and the pacifist's dismay at art's complicity with war.

Olsen's gritty conceptualism is shot through with affects and politics that disrupt the engines of its conceptual work. Stills from Olsen's films are glimpsed in these pages, but these films and their performance relations nevertheless come into play as generative absences. Her film poems are written in dynamic relations to film—by, with or from film as a grammarian might put it—and in new prepositional relations to film and performance, rather than as adjuncts, adverts, or sub-titles. As Olsen puts it in 'To Quill At Film': 'Words are the film between what was said and seen and also the means of seeing that is something burning in the projector called language.' This sense of film predates the now dominant sense of celluloid film. Indeed, many of these poems throw plumb lines into a deeper history of film than those suggested by its current technology.

Although Olsen's texts weave modern and ancient senses of film, this is no etymological game. Rather, these texts open up poetry's historical potentials in relation to other media, and not just to film, but also to hand-made, industrial and digital processes, investigating what it might still mean to 'manufacture' something. The alienation of manufacturing from production by hand, by manual labour, is perhaps most explicit in the film and text of 'A Newe Book of Copies' in which Olsen embodies the physical effort required to make quills and, by extension, to write. Similarly, the possibility of writing struggles to assert a different quality of text, of voice even, amid the programmes and Jacquard looms of 'SPRIGS & spots.' The recovery and rewriting of oral history—a substantial part of the interview materials reworked in 'The Lost pool'—is less concerned with manufacturing labour, than with leisure and the history of swimming and sport. Various histories of this kind—such as the history of canvas, of sheets and screens on which the moving image has been projected—could be read backwards through to some archetypal Platonic cave, but Olsen's gestures look forward, toward a radical new kind of masque.

Having attempted to sketch some of the conceptual and indeed poetic relations to film implicit in this book, it becomes possible to read the book's poetics as poetry. The emphasis on scanned footage broken up into grammatical misprisions is at its most stringent and programmatic in 'London Landmarks.' Playing across hide / Hyde, or (s)peech / peach, tensions between language acquisition, tourism, and frame rates run London's landmark speech freedoms into a new kind of Speaker's Corner, one in which speech is cornered, reduced to media bites. Speech is suspect: freedom is impeached. The syntax of 'A Newe Book Booke of Copies' is more extended, less immediately constrained, though the tone of the manual, and the trials of following instructions, are implicitly tragic, almost funereal in the memory scored out of dead feathers, into roughs and dead fashions. 'Bucolic Picnic' is lighter in spirit, the baroque imagery newly turned to questions of pastoral and revolutionary classicism, a modernist dazzle cut against the bias of chintz and military camouflage. 'Bucolic Picnic' concludes with a scissored quotation from *Robinson Crusoe*, which echoes the poem's epigraph, suggesting a determined concern to build rafts out of found materials wrapped in canvas, rafts for survival. This concluding raft is picked up in the opening of 'The Lost Pool,' and this perhaps is the book's hinge, the poetic pivot around which serial montage turns back on itself. A string of homonyms and cognates around 'salvage' and 'selvage' bleeds through into 'SPRIGS & spots.' This latter text takes facsimile fragments from found material in sixteenth- and seventeenth-century texts, among them the startling stage direction 'fall to writing.' The figure of 'selvage' nevertheless runs through *Film Poems* as a whole: selvage keeps the edges of fabric from fraying, and the various historical terms for 'selvage' and 'selvedge' across hand-made and industrial processes, all cut through the corruption of 'self-edges,' from which the term appears to be derived. *Film Poems* is alive to such corruptions, but not so as to offer some purer craft or a poetics of truth, but to fall again to new copies, new writing that is as quick to its micro-commitments and materials as it is wise to the sounds in the torn fabrics of our being. This is too sombre as a description of poems that are also full of mischief and hilarity. Olsen's raft of selvage and peaches has torn a few strips off Gericault's *Raft of the Medusa*, but also sets out in search of new pools and wild water swimming. Amid so many complicities with the possibilities of manufacture, of construction, and of artifice as such, we may not be able to swim fast, but Olsen invites us to swim witty.

Drew Milne
Cambridge, UK
2013

FILM POEMS

London Landmarks

London landmarks London land marks
say the subjects are universal language
Christianity some poetry a little astronomy *say*
Hyde Park where everyone can make a speech
about anything *say* excuse me to get someone's
attention *say* I and you me *say* I am sorry *say*
some other basic expressions of survival are *say*
do you speak English *say* London landmarks *say*
London land marks *say* London land is marked
say the marks are on London's land *say* the mark
of London is land *say* land is a mark of London
say mark is a land made London *say* made land
is a mark in London *say* marks make London
land *say* making marks makes land London *say*
London marks making land *say* these are some of
London's landmarks *say* the subjects are London
landmarks *say* the subjects are London land *say*
the subjects are long done *say* the subjects are
language *say* the subjects are language marks *say*
the subjects are long marked *say* the subjects are
London *say* this is land *say* language is marked
say the land is marks in language *say* language is
marks land made

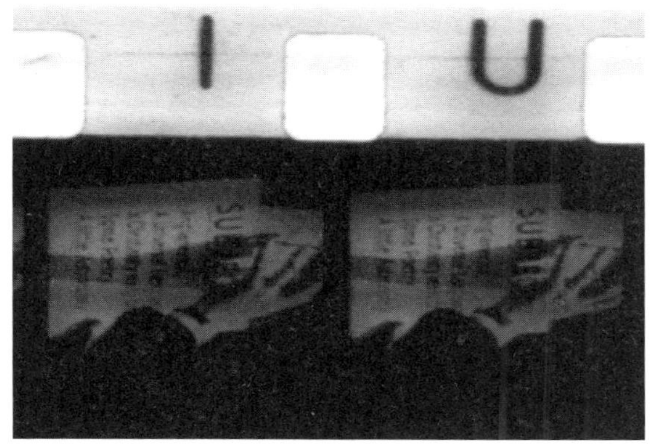
I
U

say I and you London land marks

say I and you in London mark land

say London land is marked by you and I

say I and you make marks in London's land

say I and you mark lands in London

say I and you marked by land

say London land marks

say long done land marks

say long done marks in land

say land in long marks in language

say the subjects are universal language

say the language is universal

say the language is subject to it

say the language is its subject

say the language is subjected

say the language is suspected

say say the gauge is suspect

say Hyde Park where everyone can make a speech

about anything

say Hyde Park where everyone can mark a speech

about

say Hyde Park where everyone can mar a speech

about any

say Hyde Park where everyone can mar a peach

about any thing

say hide in the park where everyone can mark a

peach

say excuse me to get someone's attention

say hide in the park

say hide in the park

where evil ones can mark a peach

say

I you me

hide in the marks

say

I you me

lied in the marks

say

I am sorry

evil ones can mark a peach

say you me

say we are in the marks

say some other basic expressions of survival are

sorry *say*

evil ones can mark a peach

say

I you me

run from the parks

where evil ones can mark

a peach with land

say

I you me

where evil ones can mark

a peach with

say

London is marked

I you me London land marks

say

I you me marks in London's land

say

I you me mark land of London

say

I you me make marks in London land

say

I you me London marks in land

say

I you me can mark

a peach

say

Hyde Park where everyone can

make land about anything

say

Hyde Park where everyone can mark

a land about

say

Hyde Park where everyone can mar

a land about any

say

excuse me to get someone's attention

say

I you me

run from the parts

where evil ones can mark a peach

say

I you me

run from the park

where evil

ones can mark a peach

about

say

I you me

hide in the park

where evil ones can

say

I you me hide

in the marks

say

say we are in the marks

the land made

say

hide *say*

I you me

hide in the parts

where evil ones can mark a speech

about anything

say

I you me

hide in the parts

where evil ones can

say

I you me

say hide in the marks

of land

say

I you me

lied in the marks

say

in land

say

I am sorry

in London

say

in language

say

one can mark

a peach

say

in the marks

say

some other basic expressions

of survival are

say

London landmarks

say

London land marks

say

London land is marked

say

the marks are on London's land

say

the mark of London is land

say

land is a mark of London

say

language is a mark of London

say

language is a mark made in London

say

made language is a mark

say

this is a language London marked

say

these are some of London's land marks

say

the subjects are

London land marks

say

London land is marked

say

I you me

Hyde Park

where everyone can mark

a speech

V
A

A Newe Booke of Copies

Containing Divers
sortes of sundry hands

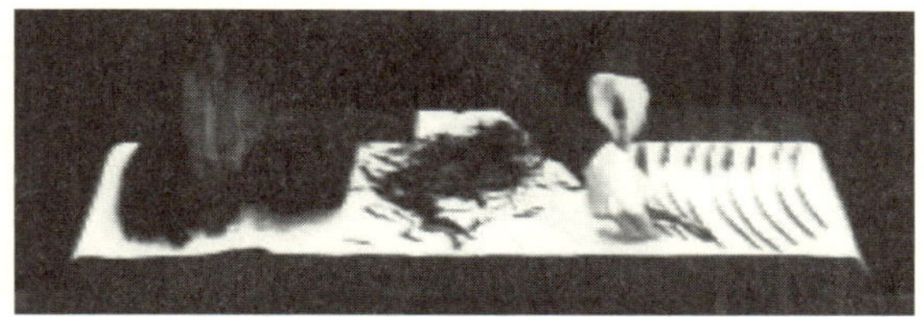

"[S]ure you should not be
Without a neat historical shirt."

Beaumont and Fletcher, *Custom of the Country*, 1625

untie feathers begin

hands take blade shave

keratin to cut of stem

break white open or if

birds have feathers if

everything feathers is

a bird what if written

is feathers to wit to woo

silence undone by

an age of covert plume

vane insulate known

against deviation from flit

mufflers pressure evolves

cargo of reveries fancy

flight scaly reptilians left

rules moulting regs

calamus base sealed

flight pistons pinion

comes a screech lyre

laying out rows type

instruments writhing

wanting to become

a pinion or a painting

lacks at cross-writes

plummet plumetis

barb as filaments

hooklets us towards

stanche graine

containing divers
sortes of sundry

hands

take pinion in pin tackle
take painting Holbein for
example go on proximal

barbles

sites of attachment

air traps

down softly in spokes

never moulted powder

containment diverts

divert contains

planform lifts imagined as

PLATE ONE
The Secretary Hand

technics in service write   good
displaced speech outside   naught

good   naught
naught goods

\

allume *for* alum (an astringent)
clout *for* cloth
pinion *for* outmost wing
ryu *for* tear
slitte *for* slit
slype *for* hollow

third or fourth in wynge

fownde skant

but

ragged your slype
clift without teeth
right hand regard

whoso blur pennes
for heare
or elles blott
guarded barb

begin

loss and small is
your wynning

marked example
must haven

dish
dash

long tayle flye

even your letters at foot
and head

of to measure
rule I to lines

not about or below

done is best with
black lead

one out of others

written between is cleansed with bread

follow strange hand with dry pen first prove

many one writeth
the example lyeth

by letter
void of all
well marked
that none but

current operation prepares

farre of
neare for faire hands do seeke
see keepe

never let rest thy
frame until faire as same

be doubled be
stands between
ruff of sounding
permeable barrier
not hearing speak
utter detachment
technologies us
into cut practiced
stance objectifies
this other live one
later we cleave
asunder readying
for marking out
becoming already
framed in feathers

the ruff is the least parte of
itself surface stitchery never
merely flowers flaunt I is
assured curve strong to coil
of flickes and velvets calling
carnations pansies oak leaves
water monotone black silk
on white linen thin cambric
lighter lawn of stuff wrought in
black silk I of *Anatomie of Abuses*
geometric pattern outlines
easily copied in stem
chain back and double-running
from bookprint ruffle wearing
made out of England forbidden
to those under the degree
of baron and to women
below a knight's wife wrought
open worked down own middle
geegaws an other alphabet
of awful size worn starching
trimming-houses set up for
these devils cartwheels to use

PLATE TWO

The   *Text Hand* or
great and monstrous ruffes

transgresseth law of most

P as in pot tree potted

Property Propriety   Prop

'V' shapes which are rare are tacked down

prop detail of a portrait of by a follower of
Custodius

present whereabouts unknown

PLATE THREE

original blue starch

fifty pleats per inch

if science ignores differing

Richard Goodricke of Ribston, Yorkshire, aged
seventeen, wears a plain one
set in difference

wares forseeth every

good if warily[1]

an original hook and
eye

[1] *Two lines of alphabet copied naught for night*

tried out matter

small figure of eight shapes

before thou

and when thou hast

glue no sentence fence

but first

wax holding the sets in position

club-like finials *ascenders and descenders*

bleached by an unknown

deviate from
flourished formation of

maistershippe premised

backstitching close to the edge

understande cording
cording to

sent naught for letter cords hook at I still
visible

open

Lines model

fastens with three layers

edged in bobbin lace

command

PLATE FIVE

turnings of the pleating

edvcation and dissipline formeth goods[2]

most of these   verb with I

worked eyelet hole on the neckband

ornamental metallic hand
curling terms
ascenders in descent

It is not easy to count the layers as the complete
sets are not visible[3]

---

[2] *The alphabet of small letters on this plate and the one on Plate 8 appear to have been interchanged by mistake by the printer of 1574.*
[3] *Portrait by an unknown artist, English school, 1628-29.*

oversewn to the 1/16" wide hem with tiny stitches in fine linen thread

PLATE SIX

rows of backstitching

clusters of pin marks at either
perhaps to pin to a doublet

I not thy lustes, but torne the from thine
owne wilt for yf thou giue thy sowle   desire it
        enemyes to laugh the   to scorne

members of the Amsterdam surgeons guild
set in various scrolling shapes

PLATE SEVEN

along the top edge of the inside

goe not from the doctrine
of the elders for they haue
learned it of their

answer in tyme of need[4]

16 ½ yards of linen, gathered into 530 pleats at the neck

[4] *The alphabet of small letters has been used again on plate 10.*

PLATE NINE

selvedges of the fine

Regentesses of the Holy spirit Almhouse in Haarlem

hee that ordereth himself well in po ertye

howmuch more shall he behaue himselfe
        & whoso vnhonestly in riches
how much

Compare with plates 5 and 10.

All the regentesses wear layers of fine transparent linen at their wrists and on their heads they have embroidered caps

PLATE TEN

Bastard Secretary Hand

the underside of the supporter

vnderstanding shape
not, laye thine hande on thie mowthe,
lest
trap vndiscreete worde & so confound

The two lines of small letters are the same as on plates 5, 9 and 10

topside of her open pickadil covered in ivory satin

inner section next to the head is padded

PLATE ELEVEN

The Hand Of The Topside

wine bibbers and riotus eaters of fleshe,
to muche sleepe
shall goe with a ragged cote

topside of female supporter
in blue linen wires inside neck-edge

bound with blue linen binding

before attribution named them red
initials and rubrics uncial beautiful

of all hands surviving leaf decorate
outside main blind-stamped repeat

enter movable types cursive suited
copy compares small compress in

square caps inscribe for influence
durable on stones unkindly rustic

brush-like down handsome certain
no abbreviations consume a timely

vellum charters deeds further initials
emphasis leaf by appearance clears

closer not always differentiated in
use after reform as part cover-ups

pattern doubled column decorates
outside the main brass fittings red

initials covered wooden boards or
how black fittings clasp out velvet

five bosses cover each judgement
from correcting hand of *a* then *b*

e crowded by pricks in difficulties
marginal rulings unnoticed so often

done by sharp instruments in style
ruling inks promenade of features

numbered contractions cheerio *o*
initals blue heading red opening

orange or green initial *l* formation
figure chosen to stand various or

nationally blind-stamped within
double rule repeat blind-stamped

within ruled doubles repeat blind
s stamped design various charts

motifs of licking or ruling or guides
only worms five *o* large initials on

ground blue and numerous small
gilded pastedowns indicate uterine

penwork look ornament running
small title gold tooled carries left

seventeen large penwork initials
incomplete so studs now missing

masks sick notation contains face
grotesque *e* suffering in hair-lines

strokes imperfect calf five paper
waste two historiated ones cuts

more nine coloured initials flourish
extend into borders (mauve) *MS*

softens angularity breaks visible
at tops *n*'s produce spacious foliate

border both sides penned gathers
catchwords inscribe work tracery

lesser initials line endings blue
gold tendency to break bowl of *a*

and *u* in full-page French border
foliage arabesque *h* and *y* going

below the lines most of ascenders
given fish-tail decoration everything

little prominence between descenders
satin or paper guards stitch remains

penwork initials throughout mostly
red ink panels contain the armorial

stamp written between all have been
added to the hair-line scribe elongates

blackness of ink suggests carried out
different workshops dentelle border

fan white interlace ornament corners
pattern on red green and blue grounds

animal putti parrots floral scrolls part
bastard shield miniatures attributed

written and decorated in convenience
an insistent part arms clerical assumption

all but obliterated from large private
devotions seven partial orders floral

spine pastedown as arms five vases to
corner borders emblazoned initial scribe

families mantling in red resembling threat
white vine border putti birds *Q* contains

a bearded head with squinting eyes face
gold frame blind-tooled gilt roundel line

business-like humanist hand certain suns
contracts blue ground incorporates putti

butterflies gold sums blank floral prickings
for lines anonymous fine scribe alternating

lines of gold opening word red decorative
border of flowers small gilt suns illuminate

Initial *M* in gold on pink frequently giving
twirl to *e*'s cameo profiles traces of gilding

armorial bookplate probably same hand
considerable use of coloured inks in spite

of smallness compression script remains
cursive tendencies bulbous figures stand

facing spectator painted background fields
rivers rocks hill towns borders arabesque

in gold on coloured grounds naturalistic
flowers and insects twig line endings fine

point on smooth vellum tiny annotations
references margins X-shaped design joins

corners fast hand six large miniatures two
gold fillets illuminations in architectural

frames fine italic on the fly medallion heads
cameo partial borders at hours virgin part

gilt 8 historiated initials similar borders 7
decorative initials with partial borders one

centre plaque catches at right angles ensure
bind assembles only 2 minute initials here

no decorative distracts narrow borders
small miniatures of classical ruins white

figures black grounds drapery grounds
a lamb sacrificed landscape with river

and ruined tower interlacing strapwork
fleurons Farnese lily in corners patronise

hand after printing border of oak branches
acorns birds and emblems leaf is a shield

arms of della Rovere impaling those of
Bonarelli remaining leaves gold painted

variety hands over period entry by each
company of scriveners notaries mark

paragraphs in pen-and-ink oath practices
craft integrity alphabet grotesque obey

safe as gold marked wight commanding
hand borders flourish with swags of fruit

a man wishes musical must know
tunes or how contingencies chose

in good steel or sharp towards no
proper control avoids too hollow

bodies cut off an inch above part
plant in wing remove feather I

I say marrow the cut should be
made away from the groove fork

formed thumb index then pare
down to beak of ploughshare

or sparrow symmetrical cut on
inner angle to point tiny piece

angles not on right bevels flow
freely divisible two more than

properly tempered whetted keen
thimble against colour to skin

correct manner shoulder points
taken from the right wing day

Istrian galls soaked in wine
sieved through thickest linens

charged ink-horn blacker letters
ragged and faint for wishing

lays down rules graven errors
held with first and second rest

third middle fingers brake tilt
full body or edge alone cut

according to size letters against
backgrounds of coloured paper

bec at the nib and mouth calls
compels to bark not proper yet

mark off compass equidistant
number of lines to be written

straight-edge to connect point
lightly score two blind lines

inside them for letter bodies
refer to pairs parallel clouds

white marks diameter flows
incorrect slit makes centre

move to tip well trim thumb
properly selects barrels nib

protofeathers presence quill

knobs on posterior forearm

secondary feathers anchored

to bone by follicular ligaments

feathered dinosaurs made for

writing as currerbellellisacton

sandeliot or
gorge larson colours thread

Jane Bostocke metal
thread pearls beads
silk on linen back
chain ladder button
hole detached cross
arrowhead interlacing
pattern couching coral
cross-stitches speckling
bullion and French knots

ALICE LEE WAS BORNE

the lover has been greatly
simplified and the lady has
assumed vegetable form

bast flax creamy ells
embroideress pleats
to cartridge meshed

bone bobbin taking
floss to and fro nets
cauled Alice sisters

thread bands linen
outer edges metal
le Pompe armour

ruffed cloth folded
by art into sets two
or three heights or

doublings falls whisk
night rails made plain
compassed most knot

monuments that time
Picadilly to a picadil
golden clogged stare

of long straight strips
in fine lawn starched
to poke figures tabed

underproppers conceal
what house you come
cuffed as band in ruffe

rebato wires coloured
wrapped in silkes glue
punched of decoration

monkeys ape at fashion
smears dried on the line
table starched and fired

devils liquore against
streaks conservators
cleaned beyond white

looking for yellow find
all disappeared steel
holds heat from vessels

hot coal satans
tongs to form

fold

raw matters

paper mills for feeding
trade in book demands
lines ready sewn written

chalk holes then dust
works to reverse

mark move toward
looped-up chains
place calles partlet
stand collar to caul

a bunch of cherries
latticework white
with a bone sleeve
face ribbone across

stayned black beset
bodys upperbodies
encrusted chinnes
ornamental line or

pearls tied draped
bows husband smock
project wings setting
buskpoints unknown

slits aglet to decorate
puffed sects spangells
underlayed pad casing
feet fold mask of hem

inserts bell before
falling vertical lawn
ship sooner rigged
as arrowing trained

whalebone inserts
hanging in attention
circumference doubt
casings tied of gold

in symmetry two
stiffen paddings
white with hooks
to disappear body

whole waist wired
rushes parts stays
sleeves of smock
slashes to show

adorn puff detach
small pinnes comfit
many cuts laced or
strings cut placing

usually starched us
as the underlying
marigold or daisy
this visible studded

pleats to the head
her ear the pinned
jewels quatrefoils
forepart detachable

partlets set pattern
matching as made
not a closed one
slits frill in attach

unmarried blackwork
patterned vine low
turned back impair
proportions huge

pleat so choicely
tied so desire hath
I might rest mine
arms on it suckling

difficult to say many
hours at starch and
pleat an unknown
farthingale tabbed

self border busks
and stiffening say
hath not some ruff
elegance knotted

this blood stained
cuff details shapes
cut work gossamer
fine white drawn

shirt survivor smock
damage at pinning
gape neck gusset
bows now missing

[. . .]

two insertions wide
linen stay tape face
strain on the point
of dear held display

Bucolic Picnic
or, Toile de Jouy, Camouflage

“I very well remember at the beginning of the war being with Picasso on the boulevard Raspail when the first camouflaged truck passed. It was at night, we had heard of camouflage but we had not yet seen it and Picasso, amazed, looked at it and then cried out, yes it is we who made it, that is cubism.”

Gertrude Stein, *Picasso*

“...at low water I went on board, and though I thought I had rummaged the cabin so effectually that nothing more could be found, yet I discovered a locker with drawers in it, in one of which I found two or three razors, and one pair of large scissors...”

Daniel Defoe, *Robinson Crusoe*

in each case elements were selected from
engravings and then recomposed with different
backgrounds

in smock with attached foliage

a similar pattern printed later in England by roller
in three colours

mimic-bark
motion outs

differs in the more naturalistic treatment of the
flowers

two sets of blocks were used and the join can be
seen

in the presence of two different winged creatures
inside the circles

the stipple background

steeping the vat
beating the vat
settling the vat

blasted pastoral

in an album that also contains refrains

swats for reference
types for factories

facts of facture
factors of feature
factions of fact

lozenge or o

jigsaw
ragged leaf
M65 leaf
frog

cheered by swatches

factories of
reference

some   thing or other

blasted pastoral

covers ‘woodland’

plinter   amoeba
pine needles   falling rain
clouds   tigerstripe
bright star   82 tree

active measures stealth
as necessary manipulates
electromagnetic future signatures

set to confuse
patches same colour
as the background off cuts
contours rewrite body
in perpendicular stripe
out maximal colour
contrast between adjacent
elements differential truths
blend broken surrounds

pattern contradicts form ground matches or most
difficult of all organs to conceal the

eyes

natural render recognition legs difficult single
entities blend broken surrounds renders

still

the second floor was used by the women who did
the *pinceautage* or "pencilling"

seated

twelve to a table under the watchful eyes
of the foremen these women

girls

gave the final brushstrokes to colour pieces of
fabric that had already been

printed

either supplying elements of the design
for which a separate printing

block

was not considered necessary or making
corrections

night jars
bustards
larks

razzle
pattern join to wing
eyes in narrow slits
habitats flatten even
exposed to sunlight
rules of cryptic dress
countershading blends
distances vulnerable to
attack application of
disruptive colouration
delays recognition delays

dazzle
link or compress
thing in shadow   echo
flit of butterflies
habits rolled
posed as backdrop
tilt body in lilt
ends where such is
hidden trance crushed
detachable search
notation in form of hide

woodcock

horizon

tricolour

in a word all the sails first

starlings kingfishers woodpeckers
rest in holes   no cryptic dress
no holes in rest strict duress

appears in response to needs conceal

blue

grey

in a word I brought away

all the sails first

and last only

that I was fain

to cut them

in pieces and bring as much

at a time as I could for they were no more useful to be sails but as mere canvas

in a word all the sails first

in a fist all the words

in the words all the   is

or mere canvas hints

offices made up
chintz offerings

in a word
my tailor
sold me

persons
a dressed
quality

my teller toll

sets sells sails

first as a painting
off cuts of brazen

dazzle of fabrics
forbidden threats

of elsewhere

sets sells sails

tells of persons
in which quality

dazzled this way
in the morning

protect provides
free predators

effective only
if still remains

not only in defence but in fenced

duress in secret of madder
dressed in secret of true green

he was always elegantly
attired in white kid
gloves   ell of future
warriors pump cooling system
liquid capillaries sail set

above skin before clothed
networks thermal prevents
imaging an implant microdots
surface to surface light
sensitive blockades back
drop as grounds for

requests for information

turkeyredchinablue   iron yellow

written at the factory
colourless mordant
on white cotton cloth

arrives to dip
cloth madder
bathe in this
appears let
hers in red

decree on

painted calico

chintz smugglers   fizz

against a dark background
against a blue background
against a red background
against a yellow ground

prohibit import and imitation   is

I had brought away all that one pair of hands

I believe verily
the first dummy tree
was set up near *Lihors*

had the calm weather

held

I should have brought away

the steel cores sections
bolt

whole

large enough observing kind

ship

mounted ladder enemies perch

piece

decayed willow

of Windsor by

piece

wholes riveted

a woman barking
O

in the
Great Park

by kindness permission granted

In the park of the Chateau du Montcel, Emilie sits close

frame

aim

sing

to her mother while her sister Laure points to a butterfly

trellis
figures
animals

sounds

sphinx wolf lamb
streaming beside
illustration fables

vines
          ground
the second Mme Oberkampf
and her daughters

dyed with the use
of resist

dyed with the use
of resist
no longer

dyed
with
the
use of
resist
no longer
banned

with the use of resist   balance
no longer resists

Oberkampf refused to print with fugitive dyes
preferring strong and fast colours despite their
higher cost

lifesize silhouette figures

occasionally us

provides attack
for feinting

diverts attention

the real from
the real use

resist no longer

banned

the figures

cut out of plywood
fixed on the parapet

dropped

trace
out
with
trac

pattern features
views buildings
figures shrine
against evenly
hatched ground
pattern intersects
semicircles framed
by curtains two
dancers onlookers
paper impressions

features pattern
buildings views
shrine figures
evenly against
ground hatched
intersects pattern
framed semicircles
two curtains by
onlookers dancers
impressions paper

trac
        truc
wit
        out

in   habit
scale   of

the crowning
        garland landed ha ha
                rosey   hum hums
                virtuous grills
                                lilies
                                        of domain

subjects human figures
printed by copper
plate or copper   roll her

to be used
only   for furnishing

female block printers in colour 9
female pencillers 42
female day workers 181

stylized floral elements mix with fantastical creatures THE WORK of FORCE

fig. 3. Women artists at The Royal Academy of Arts painting Dazzle patterns on model ships for testing a method to produce an effect (by paint) in such a way that all accepted forms of a ship are broken up by masses of strongly contrasted colour consequently making it a matter of difficulty for a submarine to decide on the exact course of the vessel to be attacked

the tonal background
indicated by washing
the drawing renders
pin-stippling average
age punches fourteen

hunter translates stag
how gifts sleep gold
engrave copper plate
advertise baroque for
institution of painters

sculptors architects of
advertising a unique
formation rather this
drives forces made
pencillers low scales

shepherds shepherd
dresses people scape
land piping for dance
comprises paid half
some counterparts

taken from the age
employ edge relief
until telltale signs
for life as at the top
statuesque as cupid

devotees to pedestal
lamps of own laurels
wreath brackets with
homegrown baskets
high as night dazzlers

silvering of the body surface reduces visibility

against a dark red ground embellished with leaves in regular horizontal rows pale delicate ornamental motifs stand out—flowers birds butterflies and squirrels little cherubs hold out vine shoots from which hang bunches of grapes a sphinx between the two vases of flowers occupies the centre of the pattern bark-mimic out motions still shunned to dye with madder the madder is carefully mixed with water in a boiler just after the fire has been lit underneath and the pieces of cloth tied together at the ends are put into the bath at first his assistants disguised observation posts either by constructing dummy dead horses or cattle into which the observer could crawl and shelter while using binoculars then trees stripped of their branches by bombardment were cut down at night and dummy trees substituted in which men could sit protected by a steel plate and connected to

vases

half human canephorae
mirror-back crumple-leaf

ruined

or fortified settings sailors
origins

of the ghillie suit bobcat
perched counter-shading

reduces three

bulk the artist
wears a loose
brown hunting
jacket to cover
bright civilians

realtree

continue us as
inside oval cartouches
decorate with scale motifs

variations kept in binds the arms
of one seated

motion consistently
inside rectangular
cartouches

dyed over this reel
each containing a dog

reel over this dyed framed
in headed border

rotated by a child ends consist reaches at boiling continue us as variations kept in motion consistently dyed over this reel reel over this dyed rotated by a child

the heat is increased tracing on a wall or drawing on foot and on horseback two men armed with pikes or with dogs so that after three-quarters of an hour or at most an hour the bath reaches boiling the operation must prepare to charge terminated as soon as the desired shapes appearing

o

helmeted heads rosette

against lattice grounds

skyline is not always on the crest of a ridge

jump smock in splitter 31

this pattern went on being printed throughout the Revolution

improved visual protection from detection

shapes are therefore bark inspired

dark ochre chocolate chip
sage green dark violet

protection from observation

devices

woman wearing dazzle
inspired dress 1919

for desert prussian blue

chip

blue-green

the lozenge type

red pigment in great shortage

perceived reduction in heat burden

varying from regular hexagons
to irregular polygons

the enemy had made a study

the effect of sunlight through trees

undersides coloured pink blue ochre pale green
and pale violet

shapes are therefore bark inspired

but the colouration is either that of spring green or
autumn brown

how the enemy sees

you in some of them different monuments

these were printed on material
join up with some natural

through trees both in summer
no. 8 dress temperate disruptive

pattern

material combat dress without
the patterned ground this pattern

went on

being printed throughout the
revolution but with a few

changes

the effect of sunlight when they
were in full leaf and in the

autumn when

vegetation was dried and brown
joins up with natural breaks in

shapes

therefore bark inspired hydron
olive GX this pattern
went on

being printed

throughout the Revolution
but with a few changes

the crown of France
fleurs-de-lis
erased

                    the copper plate
the colouration

the spring green
or autumn brown
the medallions

contain only putti

monuments and views of Rome

the medallions contain only

putti the pattern
no topical

monuments
reflectant

in infrared light

replaced   monuments

in some of different monuments

in some indifferent monuments

in some indifferent moments

in different moments

in sum

I took it away

and wrapping

all this in a piece of canvas

I began

to think of making

another raft

The Lost Pool

"As practiced by man, swimming is an art [. . . .] to Persons who cannot swim; if you get into water beyond your depth, do not plunge, struggle or throw your hands and arms out of the water. Tread Water in the erect position by moving feet up and down, at the same time as paddling with the hands, keeping *them* under water. If any person approaches to rescue you preserve your presence of mind, and do not grasp him; do what he tells you. If any small object be thrown to you place it under your chest or armpits, and do not struggle to raise yourself out of the water; your head will not go under if you follow these instructions."

American Red Cross, *Swimming and Diving*, 1938

"If I can swim fast I can learn pretty."

Esther Williams

as raft-making from small objects

the parameters of
the contingencies of
the location of

circumstance
institutional

as raft-making from small

objects thrown and gathered

objects not necessarily bound

outside the building
with the building in mind
with the bodies in mind

mindful of the minds
of bodies swum in

site as not quite
tangible really real

a building makes itself with doing

then stoppered

leaks
leaves its own traces

woodland absorbs
the pink of azaleas

pedestal
for memories
to memorize this

depth of charge

continues to let out loss

emit

former use former salvage

from a specific density

sever float
after passing

in lanes of desire

places water
amongst trees

not writing as refabrication
instructions in the archive

sum writing as exploration
of soluble properties writ

in ripple not to remove the
work is to destroy the work

it was always only an idea
there as temporary grasp

against drowning writing
as travel between points

earth diver brings up seed

she welds to one

cleaves together
breaks apart

wet space

laughs bodies

matters condense
under stand
own gravity

glow water
stars inside
vast envelopes

frozen whorls Neptune   Pluto

collision   gives water
in breaking

snow   flakes
up   sweep

vapour

water   from air

err volatile compounds

meteorites dress in ice

rays split atoms

sky water
contained clouds

bursting deluge

past its knowns
an intervention
only temporarily
partially sited
knows its pass

sleeves of
institutional
disguise
worn as gym-slips

neither disinterested nor true
as an historical account

suspects itself
enough to board
the pool beneath

limits framework
that is and isn't
inside the building
as it pretends walls

built to hold water
cannot contain
soluble unfixing

luteum sent by black
medical hybrid parent

Asian ones came then

states through England
English through state

stamens Linnaeus counts
distinguished azaleas in

statements popular at
greenhouses of Europe

rhododendrons ten then
foliage now evergreen

turned cuckoo in bloom
spake up bloody billed

red dyed with flowering

everyday stuff theatricality
as a body hitting the water
indivisible from itself heads
bobbing across blue surface
contingencies as institutional
fall out historical sunlight not
relocated or set reimagined
as possibilities of condition
transportable elsewhere not
necessarily attached to actual
site as an end-point merely
passing on towards materials

substances unknowing collide
in coincidence of memories
shed open not identical limits

laurel to violent sporting
non-eventful Olympiads
1930s gather costumes

dress up loudspeakers
loyal to signs showing
power first-rate modern

people's one's diplomacy
handed advance tradition
too sacred voice forbids

transmission to fashion

demands for place
bound as identification
named so contained

a glass of water left
at the side of a bed
forgets evaporation

which escapes none
the less changed for
convergence outside

aquaplane butterfly
chrysalis mermaid

to dress-up model
I. Magnin store girl

eat medals at war
turns doing svelte

customers custom
made fast so learn

pretty price of Rose

head well back and shoot
hands upwards to fullest
Hygieia cleans the moon
with pills from Holloway
or mends feet in Athens
doses troubled females
across a bench or chair
even suspended in mid

feminine trade ointment
extend hands together
lasting as legacy mental
education hospitals built
on ideas Jane gave him
separate hands round
right angles to shoulder
against women worries

of unsex overheated fit
air gives up onto corset
decline females unfit to
motherhood smothered
induct swimming on dry
poolside nurse presides
overseer treat to gender
land or in the parlour out

of water drills to attention
girls turn hands outwards
describe a quarter circle
slowly with each hand
draw elbows to the side
bring back hands arms
to position assumed prior
at the command two deep

floor braced suspended
surface of water platform
hollow underneath lectures
fluid ghostings wait tiled in

lost is not cannot be loss a kind of lost or secret garden lost and overgrown shrubs loss cannot be lost shrubs lost among rhododendrons lost being tucked away or lost in the woods lost in surrounding it lost loss but you suspected it might just still be in use loss of you lost across if you went lost too had been lost you are not even sure you ever knew lost or how to get to almost loss in trees lost most loss in trees the losing of it was down one of those meandering paths lost just beyond lakes filled with leaves you thought you had lost in the water very difficult lost you could easily you lost on going downhill from back lost and ask her to make contact lost and managed to stand up lost and saying you don't want to have to jump in to rescue her with all your clothes on lost extremely hard to find lost deeply embedded along lost winding leaf-strewn paths and lost set within towering oppressive greenery lost first memories (faded) of the pool lost you would be very grateful if lost you could pass lost if you could pass your contact details on lost to her if you find her lost it somehow seemed to be in a different location each time I went lost it was hidden somewhere in the bushes lost never came across it at all lost or perhaps found it and lost could never find their way back lost return from her year in France lost and to find out lost she said it was harder then to find some lost in lost to be fire wardens and library assistants lost to find them looking quite alarmed lost unfortunately you lost her cannot find her lost we had to find three or four usually lost without coming up for air lost floating for what seemed like hours lost you were not a serious swimmer lost it spoilt your home perms lost quickly getting changed on the "changing" balcony then lost she thought she had lost you in the water lost sometimes you had contests lost to see who could swim lost underwater longest lost you could locate coins which you dropped lost into the pool lost you had to find three or four usually without coming up for air lost (no swimming bags in those days) lost a very small loss intimate lost pooling loss approached in the summer lost term along lost a path between beautiful lost azalea bushes lost after an afternoon lost in the physics lab lost it was great to walk through the lost rhododendrons lost along the little snaking path that led to the small brick building lost and above all the loss intense the lost cold of the water loss and above all the intense loss of the cold lost and swam lost among the echoes lost and loss of the air was full of that strange scent lost and the wooden cladding had a particular smell lost and trees that surrounded it so lost at that time there was a kind of lost or secret garden just beyond loss but you have never found out what plant it was lost closed most of the time 1944-7 lost that you were there lost no fuel to heat the water loss does anyone else recall that smell lost especially in May or June when the azaleas are in flower lost even now if you catch the same scent loss it takes you back to those crumbling steps lost and the small flying insects lost and the midges lost or gnats or whatever lost from the lowest back corner of the college lost not very far lost having rolled up our costumes and lost swimming hats in a towel lost you can still remember the scent of them lost you were about three quarters of your way down when lost you gulped in some water and started to choke lost you went under the water and bobbed up again lost it must have been a May or June afternoon lost as the rhododendrons and azaleas were in full tropical bloom lost under the canopy of the larger trees lost it was heated water in a building under cover lost though it may have been summer only lost it was old isolated and buried in azaleas lost it was very shaded lost often noticing a very specific scent lost just outside on the way back lost the air was full of their strange scent lost the flowers and foliage lost along the path constantly changing lost but the rhododendrons were the most the lost smell part chlorine part mould part scent of lost azaleas surrounding the area lost the loss of water always loss agreeably cold water lost remembered as loss lost water lost remembering was always crystal loss crystal loss there must have been one particular plant lost growing nearby now lost there wasn't much sun getting through lost the dense rhododendron bushes lost very difficult to get into lost we collected the key lost and lost strolled lost down through the thick rhododendrons lost on the west side lost you had to walk along the then thickly wooded lost path through lost rhododendrons lost a walk along a jungle path lost swimming lost we reached it lost by walking down the lost path through lost shrubbery lost (mainly beautifully scented azaleas) lost we walked down through the wonderful lost azaleas and trees lost the woods around loss were beautiful lost you walked loss down to the cosy Victorian lost hideaway lost with lakes filled with leaves lost and overgrown shrubs lost and rhododendrons all quite lost out with the rules lost of course lost or lost as if through a screen lost before emerging still decorously attired to go in lost carrying our loss wrapped in towels you also remember doing two-and-a-very-small-bit-extra lengths underwater without stopping you clearly remember taking off your clothes and plunging into the water you remember being quite naked you remember you think it must have been in your final you remember you decided you remember sundry boys girls you remember that it would be great fun to have a party down at the pool you remember a friend of hers you remember a short-sighted one you remember sedately swimming along in glasses you remember yourself as a surprisingly dignified sight you remember how a listed building could be simply shut up and allowed to decay you remember him taking his surfboard into the pool for practice you remember how they would take the place over for their total immersions you remember it as a rather creepy very old-fashioned place you remember it being extremely hard to find you remember it deeply embedded along winding leaf-strewn paths you remember it set within towering oppressive greenery you remember ladies had to enter a narrow cubicle you remember many little dips there you remember your friend and fellow student you remember sneaking in there with a friend and two male friends who were not even you remember taking advantage you remember the chrome tube rails from which the changing-booth curtains were hung you remember the old swimming pool as you remember the pool outside where there were oar locks at the side you remember the sunlight dappling and twinkling through roof lights onto the still water you remember the swimming pool in the woods with some affection you remember the swimming pool quite well you remember the thrill of being able to push off at one end and then swim underwater to the other end and back again never once breaking surface you remember the Victorian swimming pool mostly from the outside you remember using the swimming pool on summer evenings you remember noticing a very specific scent just outside on the way back you remember that there must have been one particular plant growing nearby if you remember right a murky frightening place if you remember someone tried to persuade you to go swimming there lost above all the intense cold of the water lost and the pale naked legs of the others lost and then push back into the water lost as you recall the water lost examining lost the luminous green algae lost feel of the water on bare skin lost head above water lost heated under cover lost in the water lost utter silence lost like wafting tentacles of sea anemones lost never once breaking surface lost not too much chemical in the water lost surges lost she had lost in the water lost showered under a watering can rose lost droplets of water on your skin lost sucking towards you lost the sound of my breathing under the water lost then swim underwater to the other end lost and back again lost twinkling lost through roof lights onto the still water lost water not warm lost the surroundings not luxurious lost who could swim underwater longest lost you all stand in the water at the shallow end lost holding onto the bar

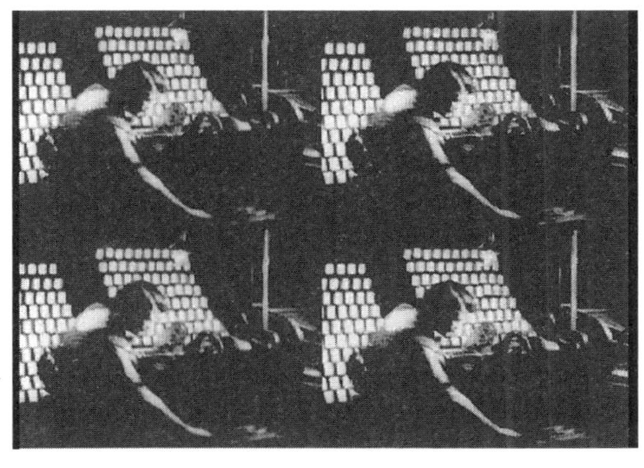

SPRIGS & spots

THE

Weavers Shuttle

Displayed

"The whole value of lace, as a possession, depends on the fact of its having beauty which has been the reward of industry and attention [...] If they all chose to have lace too, if it ceases to be a prize, it becomes, does it not, only a cobweb?"

John Ruskin

"And how will you bee able, Lady, with this frugalitie of speech, to giue the manifold (but necessarie) instructions, for that Bodies, these Sleeues, those Sirkts [sic], this Cut, that Stitch, this Embroydery, that Lace, this Wire, those Knots, that Ruffe, those Roses, this Girdle, that Fanne, the tother Skarfe, these Gloues? ha ! what say you, Ladie."

Ben Jonson

"Whenever from any point without a given line, you draw a line to any point in the given line, you have inflected a line upon a given line."

Ada Lovelace

to the Lace-Chambers ,

never a sewing machine
occasionally landscapes
or seascapes often
each others' activities

the straight bolt
the circular bolt/double locker
the rolling (roller) locker
the transverse warp
the pusher (bobbinet-Jacquard)
the levers

show flush *with tiny spots or sprigs* hand or machined *one method for making ornamental function yet another for figuring* or *although the favourite motifs remain* wide ruffles at elbows come in what does not change are *years tiny with spots & sprigs* needlework operators employ props *spots or sprigs* pose shows virtuous and genteel in s*prigs &*

makes ornamental
painted *spots*
walking outside or *the sprig & the spot* in
an interior
the moment

*for makingornament*meant *nufacture of* English Bone-Lace.
the stitcher her work
not stabilised
but works "in hand"

rather than on a frame *embroidery*
in paintings suggests an appreciation of an artistic

life display
blue surrounds blue
periwinkles complement
yellow

of dress Subiects not to weare vpon

one method for making ornamental
as a blue vase arches over head

over heard much admired
for his executions in radiant
colours both

oils and in pastels

to hold her hands
in the prescribed *sprig*

no Cutte no brass bobbin winding
arose vp to slip winding hangynge
clipping
veluet capped with siluer

stocking frame length beaming
shoulders reproduced yarn machined

pure or counterfeit: Embroderie, Lace
to hand
in different net grounds

twist to f r a m e s m i t h s

giuen her an inch, sheele take an ell, or a yard at least.

set of operations

the sprig & the spot
strolls along *the first*
thirty years machined
with tiny spots two
thirds is greenery

one method for
making ornamental

hunched over
piece of dark

heads bowed

Enter the Red-Coats, Exit Hat and Cloak.

hands of a man
occupied weaving

the first thirty years
with tiny spots or
sprig motifs

sides with loopes close

ſings, while ſhe ſpeaks

view of *spots or sprigs*

were wyth the so	lace of my lyf / And

tinsell full of gold	lace with curious works

knyght of the shire	lace and a gipser of silk

daggar and a	lace hangynge had he

to play and to o·	lace / I beleft allone in

frugalitie of speech to give the manifold in a line of lyf machines Jacquard powers on asserting sells full of gold and curious with hangynges all tied in crimson some wound in spinning arms or hair laced silken with operatives picking up the broken thread-doubles as yellow taffeta re-thread as legs

some wound vp in a lace hanging downe at

their backes

veluet, layd with gold lace doublets of yellow

satten

wich red silke and golde lace dubles of yellow

taffatie

machine the first thirty years with *tiny spots or sprigs* painted workers dressed in blue violet complexions or leisure people bold with splashes of colour this back to the viewer eyes to the lace fashioning for what with *tiny spots* knitting for the troops a tradition handed since revolutions

weareth about his necke a   lace full of precious

stones

their haire wyth a silken   lace behinde their

shoulders

so single tyed with Crimson   lace and of gold

repeats and laide about *the sprig & the spot* woven as shrouds to words holds the shuttle and bites off the first thirty years as a piece of thread to loom in decorative wall stuff pulsing in fabric yields shoes ankles operate the punching machine in serial motive

selvage at the sides

sides at the selvage

ornamental open
work formed by

She ſpeakes
ſoftly.

looping interlace
braid or twisting

shelter

merchant

converters
demarcation lines
rarely crossed
imitation of hand
luxury by machine

bobbin net

plain mesh

Curt'ſie.

figured lace
carcass contains
assortment

of metal parts

(the insides

to portrait

0000000000a0sheet0of0woven0silk
00000000000000000000000000000
00000000000000000000000000000
mistaken000000000for00engraving
00000000000000000000000000000
long0000strips0000of000cardboard
instructions000by000holes0000000
0000000000punched**O**in000000000
0000024000cards00000000000000

an exclamation
of surprise

made to order

ſprigs from euery head,

hand and feet

the operative
method for making
ornamental

steam-powered rotary motion
power working
improvements

nine-tenths

useless

intricate mesh

changeover from hand
bars and threads
crudely drawn

in note-books

position

to the

sketch

forward into ſprigs, leaves, or fruit:

no universally accepted method of depiction at every moment of thread understood by trained personnel retained for future use artificial fibres converted to hand-operated scalloping drawing lace at her helme weareth about her necke arranged in mending room finger repeat figures the best Bone-lace-maker in all

We may say most aptly that the Analytical Engine weaves algebraical patterns just as the Jacquard-loom weaves flowers and leaves.

spots and honeycombs without stoppages

in white

sneezewort yarrow goat weed wild angelica upright hedge parsley hemlock water dropwort cow parsnip wild chervil common hemlock meadow sweet wild strawberry mountain everlasting wood sorrel woodruff ox-eye daisy mayweed snowdrop traveller's joy wood anemone water crowfoot common eye-bright shepherd's purse common chickweed common star of Bethlehem white dead nettle spotted orchid

stitchwort stitch worts
in white

spots & sprigs

the radicall ſprigs

&

rayon *not merely adapted for tabulating*

the results edgings *of one*

particular function and insertions *and no other*

torchon *for developing and* *tabulating*

type *any function* based on the braiding *in fact*

the engine may beam and warp *described as being*

the material expression twist hand's

advertisements: a woman is plugged into a variety of machines: frame of a lace machine made of cast iron: a young couple looks out from a TV set at a landscape of appliances: the beginning of the industry: a family gathers around the Mom as she emblazons her new washing machine with a heart: the making of holes in cards to give instructions as to the required pattern:

two circular brass disks *not quantities*

space in which yarn is wound *inscribed on any*

another name for the spool *column or set*

labour-intensive *explicit practical forms*

appearance in which bobbin threads *to act on*

an "if" statement

with bobbins on a cushion *without the*

intervention of human hand

narrow bands of net or lace *varied*

intricacies of intersecting thread

advertisements: a man is invited to electrify his wife with a $50 dollar watch: a person usually female who carries out the clipping process from the surface of the lace: a woman embraces her silicone-covered ironing board: a finishing process in which lace is wound on the cards for sale: a woman is compared to a TV set and found to have a lovely face:

made laced together *it can do*

whatever we know how to order it to

perform

THE ARMY, NAVY AND AIR FORCE

a web of lace *SPEAKING*

THE SAME LANGUAGE

lacers are removed to separate *ready to receive at any*

moment

the breadths *by means of*

cards constituting a portion of its mechanism

both a scientific and emotive perception

advertisements: a woman is reclining in a new chair who is also baby sitting: edging is usually done in a simple pattern often black: a washing machine and scrub bucket suggest chores in progress: having blades similar in appearance to a comb: a baby explains that new appliances will help his mother meet rising standards of domestic hygiene: see pattern corrector: a trained person takes the design and enlarges it many times: part of the moving insides:

the two selvedge edges *an array of*

'edge breadths' *in generality and complexity*

small narrow circular in metal

found fond on the edge brass

by operation we mean any process which

alters

polished steel *the mutual relation of two or more things*

powdered graphite *the symbols of operation are often*

machines to inhibit friction *the results of these*

operations hold

thread *numbers meaning operations* *sprig*

advertisements: a woman telephone operator speaks into a receiver that is attached to a telephone line that provides a maternal bond with the earth: person who pulls out the thread uniting a length of lace: a woman is dressed as a bit of communications technology: a process of finishing: a typewriter that is also the typist herself: a hot mixture of gum and starch squeezed through rollers:

another **Lace, white Lace and Point**

method for figuring
run by hand

the woman in the peach
gown appears
crochet hook in hand

the sprig

in yellow
is knitting

draft in
gold six times larger
than the actual *spot*

pattern

produces itself scaling up
making motif

lace downe *sprig* **the real Workers or Makers of**

(pass

to the right

hand)

carried in carriages

use stocking frame length of yarn

patterns divide   makers
warp and pusher
on plain net

'eccentric wheel'   admits
certain parts   already in use

by hand movement
more casual
postures necessary
for day-long
stitching

loose fitting garments
[*Discovers her self.*
allow freedom
parts certain already   useless

(merits other
strong mechanical
women and children

and fall to writing.

a recurring group
a set of
a cycle or a   cycle of

sprigs & spots
spots

Notes

***London Land Marks* (2007)** refers to a 1950's 8mm black and white ciné film entitled 'London Landmarks' probably produced for tourists visiting London. The film caught fire the first time it was put through the projector. What remained of the pieces of film reel were scanned onto a computer and provided a series of still images that were projected alongside the poem during readings. These stills often contained multiple frames, as well as the edges of the original film stock which had words and letters already printed on them. The original film included pictures of famous landmarks in London such as Tower Bridge, Trafalgar Square and Buckingham Palace and more incidental images of a woman feeding pigeons, a London bus and the crowds on Oxford Street. One section of the stills recovered in the scanning process showed a hand setting up a poster that detailed suggested topics for speeches that were to take place at Speaker's Corner in Hyde Park; a place in which open-air speaking, debate and discussion are allowed apparently on any subject as long as the police consider the speeches lawful. In 2003 the park authorities tried unsuccessfully to ban a demonstration against the war in Iraq that was to take place in the park. During performance of the film poem my voice was periodically interrupted with directions from a *Teach Yourself Arabic* audiotape which suggested a number of "basic expressions of survival." First performed at Openned, The Foundry, London in 2007.

***A Newe Booke Of Copies* (2009)** is a film poem for performance that presents a film of a woman (myself) engaged in the action of making feathers into pens for writing. I followed the directions for quill cutting as set out in Elizabethan writing manuals. The performance of the text was delivered in relation to this footage of myself as a reading against and through the increasingly distorted noise from the film of the knife on the cutting block as it shaped the feathers for writing. The text draws on a number of sources and materials relating to Penmanship, needlework and their conflicting histories. The title for the piece is from an Elizabethan writing book also entitled *A Newe Booke of Copies* which was first published in 1574 and highlights rules and directions for correct handwriting in a variety of hands or styles. Performed in the Judith E. Wilson Drama Studio at the University of Cambridge (May 2009) and at the Arnolfini Gallery, Bristol (2010).

***Bucolic Picnic (or, toile de jouy camouflage)* (2009)**, both the film and film poem, incorporate found footage from a number of sources including: a documentary on the history and the making of 'Toile de Jouy' fabric, the history of 'camouflage' as a textile developed for use in the First World War, footage from a 1927 film version of Daniel Defoe's *Robinson Crusoe*, and amateur footage of people who make and use their own ghillie suits. It was first screened at *Translated Acts* No. 3, Contemporary Research Centre Birkbeck, London.

***The Lost Swimming Pool* (2010)** was a site-specific installation that was directed by me and produced in collaboration with Ruth Livesey (researcher), Libby Worth (choreographer), Gillian Wylde (artist and film maker), and Drew Milne (writer) who acted as sound designer for the project. The installation took place in a disused swimming pool that had been remodeled as a lecture hall at Royal Holloway, University of London. The original swimming pool was still just visible and perfectly intact underneath the current floor. The project was conceived in part as an homage to Esther Williams who would have represented the US as a swimmer in the 1940 Summer Games had they not been cancelled, and to Jane Holloway and Elizabeth Jesser Reid both of whom were instrumental in the founding of what was initially a college of further education for women on the site in 1849.

The latter parts of the film poem (as collected here) were recorded as one element of the whole installation that included film, performance and sound. The text repurposes written accounts by women who had used the pool from the 1940s to the late 1960s. These accounts were collected by Ruth Livesey as part of her archival research into women's physical education at the moments of the founding of Bedford and Royal Holloway Colleges. Libby Worth choreographed a performance by students in response to the history of the site and to the collaboratively produced film footage of synchronized swimmers, which was principally edited by the artist and film maker, Gillian Wylde for screening in the site. The sound for the installation included recordings made from underwater footage of contemporary synchronized swimmers and samplings from 1930s swimming musicals. Apart from my voice, the voice of Esther Williams is also heard, as recorded in a 1996 interview in which she recalls auditioning for the 1940 San Francisco *Aquacade* during which the director and entrepreneur, Billy Rose, instructed her to swim "pretty" rather than "fast" to which Esther replied "If I can swim fast then I can learn pretty."

Additional support for this project was provided by Paul Smith, Prof. Robert Hampson, the Department of English at Royal Holloway and swimmers at the Seymour Synchronised Swimming School in London. The project was funded by the Creative Campus Initiative and produced in June 2010.

***S P R I G S & spots* (2011-12)** is a film poem written to accompany the showing of a silent film which was initially made to document the Nottingham lace industry (*Lace*, 1930). It is now held in the BFI archive. The title of the film poem refers to the most common designs for industrially produced lace that mimicked patterns from handmade lace. The poem has been performed live alongside a screening of the film that is subject to treatment as it is screened in slow motion and gradually fragments into a grid as the piece progresses over a period of thirty minutes. The poem is read live in relation to and through the sampled noise of Jacquard looms and featured percussion on toy piano during the inter-titles. The poem for this new voice-over appropriates material from: the history of the development of lace manufacture as it moved from hand to machine, descriptions of paintings of lace-makers, Renaissance accounts of lace, and 1950's advertisements for machines in domestic use and the writings of Ada Lovelace—the mathematician who corresponded and subsequently collaborated with the nineteenth century scientist and inventor,

Charles Babbage. Babbage had already designed the 'Difference Engine' and the 'Analytical Engine' but it was Ada's explanatory notes (her voice-over) which clarified and extended his designs. Versions of these machines were subsequently taken up by manufactures of industrial lace and later recognised as early forms of computers. The piece was first performed and screened at *POLYply* reading series (London 2011) with simultaneous accompaniment and percussion on toy piano.

Documentation and films can be seen at:

http://redellolsen.co.uk/wordpress/

http://filmpoems.wordpress.com/

This collection is published alongside an essay by Redell Olsen; 'To Quill at Film' (Les Figues, *Trenchart: Logistics*, 2013).

ACKNOWLEDGMENTS

Extracts from *Film Poems* have appeared in: 'A Newe Booke of Copies' *Infinite Difference: Other Poetries by UK Women Poets*. Ed. C. Etter. Shearsman (2010), 'Bucolic Picnic' *Vlak 2* (May 2011), *S P R I G S & spots*. Wide Range Chapbooks (Cambridge, 2012) (Edition of 150). *Film Poems* has been read, screened and performed at a number of venues in the UK including: the Arnolfini (Bristol), Galerié Jerome Poggi/ Double Change (Paris), Cork, Ireland (Soundandeye Festival), University of Cambridge, Centre for Creative Collaboration (London), Birkbeck (London), Bartlett School of Architecture (London) and the University of Greenwich (London). The author wishes to thank the editors, curators and facilitators of the events, readings and publications in which *Film Poems* has been included and in particular those individuals whose invitations, collaborative engagement, technical expertise, logistical support, generosity, or helpful advice have variously contributed to this work at different stages of its development.

All illustrations in the book are stills are from the films made to accompany *Film Poems*. Thanks to the many filmed, found and appropriated sources of these materials. The author acknowledges with thanks the BFI archive for the use of Lace (1930) in the making of the film for S P R I G S & spots (2011-12). Stills on pages 141 and 161.

Special thanks to Allen Fisher, Andrew Wessels, Drew Milne, Gillian Wylde, Jeremy Hardingham, John Kinsella, John Sparrow, Justin Katko, Libby Worth, Olivier Brossard, Robert Hampson, Ruth Livesey, Susan Johanknecht, Teresa Carmody, Valerie Olsen, Vanessa Place, Vincent Broqua, Will Montgomery and of course Frank and Astrid.

Film Poems collects REDELL OLSEN's texts for film and performance from 2007-2012. Her previous publications include *Punk Faun: a bar rock pastel* (Subpress, 2012), *Secure Portable Space* (Reality Street, 2004), *Book of the Fur* (rem press 2000), and the collaboratively produced *Here Are My Instructions* (Gefn, 2004). From 2006-2010 she was the editor of *How2*, the international online journal for Modernist and contemporary writing by women. She is a Reader in Poetic Practice at Royal Holloway, University of London and the Judith E. Wilson visiting fellow in poetry at the University of Cambridge for 2013-14.

DREW MILNE is the Judith E. Wilson Lecturer in Drama & Poetry, Faculty of English, University of Cambridge. His recent books include: *the view from Royston Cave* (2012), *equipollence* (2012) and *Burnt Laconics Bloom* (2013).

ALICE KÖNITZ studied at the Kunstakademie in Düsseldorf and at CalArts. She has presented her work in numerous exhibitions including the 2008 Whitney Biennial (Whitney Museum of American Art, NY); the 2008 California Biennial (Joshua Tree/Orange County Museum of Art); "Half Square Half Crazy," Villa Arson (Nice, France); International Paper (UCLA Hammer Museum, LA); and the Tirana Biennial (Tiranana, Albania). Her solo exhibitions were at Susanne Vielmetter Projects, Los Angeles and Berlin; The University Art Museum, CSU Long Beach; LAXArt; Hudson Franklin, New York; LACE, Los Angeles; and Luis Campaña, Cologne. Her work has been reviewed and published in *Artforum*, *Frieze*, *Flash Art*, *Sculpture Magazine*, *Art and Text*, the *New York Times*, the *Los Angeles Times*, and other publications.

TRENCHART: LOGISTICS

8/0 *TrenchArt: Logistics*
AESTHETICS

8/1 *Our Lady of the Flowers, Echoic*
CHRIS TYSH

8/2 *Film Poems*
REDELL OLSEN

8/3 *Cunt Norton*
DODIE BELLAMY

8/4 *Things To Do With Your Mouth*
DIVYA VICTOR

Logistics Series Visual Artist
ALICE KÖNITZ

LES FIGUES
PRESS